Elizabeth H - Margar

D1034429

ANTIQUES A... ...IR VALUES

PEWTER

COMPILED BY TONY CURTIS

First Published	June	1977
Reprinted	Jan	1978
Revised Edition	June	1978
Reprinted	March	1980

ISBN: 0-8256-9659-3
ORDER NO.: 450004

Copyright © Lyle Publications MCMLXXVII.
Published by Lyle Publications, Glenmayne, Galashiels, Scotland.
Distributed in the U.S.A. by Quick Fox, 33 West 60th Street, New York, N.Y. 10023.

INTRODUCTION

Congratulations! You now have in your hands an extremely valuable book. It is one of a series specially devised to aid the busy professional dealer in his everyday trading. It will also prove to be of great value to all collectors and those with goods to sell, for it is crammed with illustrations, brief descriptions and valuations of hundreds of antiques.

Every effort has been made to ensure that each specialised volume contains the widest possible variety of goods in its particular category though the greatest emphasis is placed on the middle bracket of trade goods rather than on those once-in-a-lifetime museum pieces whose values are of academic rather than practical interest to the vast majority of dealers and collectors.

This policy has been followed as a direct consequence of requests from dealers who sensibly realise that, no matter how comprehensive their knowledge, there is always a need for reliable, up-to-date reference works for identification and valuation purposes.

When using your Antiques and their Values to assess the worth of goods, please bear in mind that it would be impossible to place upon any item a precise value which would hold good under all circumstances. No antique has an exactly calculable value; its price is always the result of a compromise reached between buyer and seller, and questions of condition, local demand and the business acumen of the parties involved in a sale are all factors which affect the assessment of an object's 'worth' in terms of hard cash.

In the final analysis, however, such factors cancel out when large numbers of sales are taken into account by an experienced valuer, and it is possible to arrive at a surprisingly accurate assessment of current values of antiques; an assessment which may be taken confidently to be a fair indication of the worth of an object and which provides a reliable basis for negotiation.

Throughout this book, objects are grouped under category headings and, to expedite reference, they progress in price order within their own categories. Where the description states 'one of a pair' the value given is that for the pair sold as such.

Printed by Apollo Press, Dominion Way, Worthing, Sussex, England.
Bound by Newdigate Press, Vincent Lane, Dorking, Surrey, England.

CONTENTS

ALMS DISHES

19th century circular pewter alms dish, 12½in. diam. $50 £25

A French pewter circular alms dish, the border etched "J. Gruson Roi, 1865", 12½in. diam. $80 £40

Alms dish inscribed 'the Upper Door 2', and on reverse 'St. Olaves Ch, 1718', 9¼in. diam., by John Boult. $110 £55

Mid 18th century alms dish, rim inscribed 'St. Olaves, 1757, Southwark', 12in. diam $170 £85

A circular pewter alms dish, 15in. diam. $170 £85

Late 17th century Flemish alms dish with jelly mould centre, 41cm. diam. $700 £350

A pewter baptismal bowl, etched with flowers. $80 £40

An early oval pewter shaving bowl. $200 £100

Rare, English pewter bowl, dated 1709, 6in. diam. $250 £125

Liberty & Co. 'Tudric' pewter rose-bowl, 14.5cm. wide, circa 1903. $370 £200

An early 19th century pewter Montieth bowl of Queen Anne design. $750 £375

A large, rare, pewter Montieth bowl, circa 1700. $1,600 £800

Deep-welled 'Mount Edgecumbe' bowl with broad rim, 14in. diameter, circa 1640. $2,430 £1,350

(Sotheby's)

Victorian tortoishell card case with
pewter inlay. $18 £9

A Britannia metal oval biscuit box.
$50 £25

Chinese repousse pewter medical box,
1850-60, 9in. long. $80 £40

Liberty pewter and enamel tobacco box
with sides cast with rows of stylised
leaves and set with blue-green enamel
cabochons, 4¾in. $193 £100

Mahogany cased pair of Chinese pewter
tea canisters, circa 1780. $350 £175

German silvered metal box, circa
1905, 16cm. wide. $481 £260

11

BUCKLES

William Comyns silvered belt buckle,
London 1901, 7.25cm. wide. $93 £50

Liberty and Co. Cymric belt buckle.
$116 £60

Art Nouveau belt buckle, 7.75cm. wide,
probably American, circa 1900.
$139 £75

French belt buckle, silver coloured
metal, circa 1900, 7.5cm. wide.
$370 £200

French Art Nouveau belt buckle, 7.5cm.
wide, circa 1900, gilt teeth. $407 £220

Good, Austrian, enamelled silver metal
buckle, circa 1900, 11.5cm. high.
$618 £320

BEAKERS

BEAKERS

An unusual German tapered beaker with rococo decoration in relief all around body, 5in. high. $60 £30

Dutch pewter beaker, circa 1700, 14.2cm. high, maker's mark PB.
$212 £110

BUTTONS

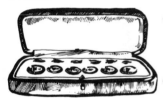

Box of six buttons with fasteners, 1920. $10 £5

A set of six Liberty and Co. Cymric buttons. $106 £55

CAUDLE CUPS

Small double-handled William and Mary caudle cup by Thomas Hicks, circa 1690. $720 £400

Rare, small, William and Mary caudle cup, 2¾in. high, circa 1690.
$900 £500

13

**Joseph A. Hodel presentation casket in silvered metal, 1906, 18.25cm.
high.** $656 £340
(Sotheby's Belgravia)

Pair of late 19th century soft metal candlesticks. $30 £15

A pair of 19th century pewter candlesticks, 23cm. high. $72 £36

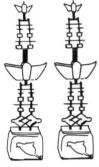

A pair of Japanese pewter pricket altar candlesticks with pierced stems, 52cm. high. $140 £70

Pair of Sheffield plate table candlesticks on rococo 'C' and 'S' scroll bases, 8in. high, circa 1845. $140 £70

Pair of pewter candlesticks, 9in. high, circa 1820. $160 £80

Pair of 18th century pewter candlesticks, 13in. high. $200 £100

CANDLESTICKS

19th century Saxon candlestick.
$460 £230

19th century Saxon candlestick in pewter.
$480 £240

WMF candelabrum, circa 1900, 27.5cm. high.
$463 £240

One of a pair of 18th century pewter candlesticks, 16in. high. $650 £325

Pair of Art Nouveau pewter candlesticks, 16½in. high. $630 £350

One of a pair of polished pewter candelabra by Henry van de Velde, circa 1898, 10in. high. $700 £350

Rare William and Mary pewter candlestick, 6½in. high, circa 1690.
$720 £400

(Sotheby's)

One of a pair of rare English pewter wall sconces, circa 1750, 11in. high.
$1,500 £750

(Christie's, New York)

Fine Stuart pewter candlestick, 8¼in. high, circa 1680-90. $2,027 £1,050

One of a pair of Gothic altar candle-holders, probably Dutch or North West German, about 1500, 26cm. high. $3,200 £1,600

Fine and rare Charles II octagonal based candlestick, 7¾in. high, circa 1675. $2,970 £1,650

An extremely rare bell-based candle-stick with central dished grease catch, 21.7cm. high, circa 1600. $4,000 £2,000

Fine quality pewter candlesticks.
                    $5,760 £3,200

One of a pair of mid 17th century pewter candlesticks, 9½in. high.
                    $17,000 £8,500

Late 18th century pewter charger with maker's mark, R.I.I. $80 £40

18th century pewter charger with deep central bowl, 13in. diameter. $80 £40

18th century Continental charger, with moulded rim, 14in. diameter. $90 £45

18th century charger with moulded rim, 14in. diameter. $90 £45

A fine 18th century pewter charger, 15in. diameter. $110 £55

18th century pewter charger, 12½in. diameter. $120 £60

18th century pewter charger with a London mark. $150 £75

CHARGERS

18th century pewter charger, 16in. diameter. $170 £85

Pewter charger, maker I.S., engraved with initials H.R.B., 18in. diameter.
$210 £105

18th century pewter charger by Christopher Cillarius. $220 £110

Early 18th century pewter charger, 19in. diamer. $260 £130

Late 17th century William & Mary pewter charger, 18in. diam.
$600 £300

22in. wide pewter charger by I. Jackson, circa 1710. $750 £375

Broad rimmed pewter charger, 18¼in. diameter, by T. Reading, London, 17th century. $864 £480

(Christie's)

Good Stuart charger by Richard Fletcher, circa 1680-85, 21¾in. diam.
$936 £520

(Sotheby's)

Charles II broad rimmed charger by Thomas Hull, 22in. diam., circa 1660-70. $1,260 £700

Fine Stuart broad rimmed charger by John Cave, Bristol, circa 1660, 20¼in. diameter. $1,296 £720

Broad rimmed pewter charger, 21¾in. diameter, circa 1675. $3,200 £1,600

Charles I 'Mount Edgecumbe' charger by Nicholas Dolbeare, Ashburton, circa 1640, 22¾in. diameter.
          $4,680 £2,600

Important Charles II broad rimmed commemorative charger by HI, circa 1662, 21¾in. diameter.
          $5,400 £3,000

A very fine commemorative charger, of English pewter, circa 1662, 55.2cm. diameter. $14,000 £7,000

Art Nouveau silvered metal clock, signed N. Bochin. $150 £75

Liberty & Co. 'Tudric' pewter clock, after 1903, 17cm. high. $176 £95

Liberty & Co. 'Tudric' pewter and enamel clock, after 1903, 18.75cm. high. $241 £130

Pewter and enamel clock, circa 1905, 14.25cm. high. $259 £140

Liberty & Co. pewter and enamel clock, 19.75cm. high, after 1903. $333 £180

Large Liberty & Co. 'Tudric' pewter and enamel clock, after 1903, 32cm. high. $888 £480

Liberty & Co. 'Tudric' pewter and enamel clock, circa 1903, 13.5cm.
high. $1,110 £600

(Sotheby's)

COFFEE POTS

A Victorian Britannia metal, vase-shaped coffee pot. $30 £15

Early 20th century pewter coffee pot with ebony handle. $30 £15

19th century pewter coffee pot, circa 1870. $50 £25

A Victorian Britannia metal coffee pot. $60 £30

A pear shaped Britannia metal coffee pot, by Dixon & Sons, Sheffield, 10in. high. $150 £75

English pewter coffee pot, circa 1840-50, 10in. high. $250 £125

Pewter hot water dish with engraved monogram.   **$50 £25**

19th century hard metal dish, 16½in. diameter.   **$60 £30**

19th century pewter hot water dish.   **$80 £40**

Pewter hot water dish with swing handles and small rectangular hinged cover in top to add hot water, by Thomas Alderson, 8in. diameter.   **$90 £45**

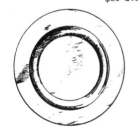

Early 19th century pewter dish, touch marks rubbed, 16½in. diameter.   **$100 £50**

An early pewter dish with moulded rim, 15¼in. diameter.   **$200 £100**

An attractive strawberry dish, the booge fluted into eighteen petal-
shaped panels, 5in. diameter, circa 1720. $560 $280
(Sotheby's)

One of a pair of oval pewter central dishes, 18in. wide, initialled RT.
$216 £120

One of four circular pewter dishes, initialled RT. $225 £125

Puiforcat stemmed dish, 6.5cm., 1930's, in silver coloured metal. $296 £160

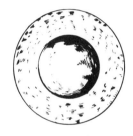

Pewter Cardinal's hat dish, French, about 1700, 15½in. diameter.
$500 £250

Part of a set of seven waved-edged pewter dishes, 9½in. across, by George Beeston. $540 £300

Charles II pewter dish by NN, 16¾in. diam., circa 1675. $540 £300

31

DISHES

Charles II broad rimmed pewter dish, 18¼in. diam., circa 1660. $990 £550

French pewter dish by R. Doirier of Paris, 16½in. diameter, dated 1677.
$1,100 £550

Elizabethan dish by IH, 12½in. diam., circa 1590. $1,116 £620

Engraved Stuart dish in pewter, 18in. diam., circa 1685. $1,350 £750

Rare 'Mount Edgecumbe' pewter dish, 12in. diam., circa 1600. $1,584 £880

Charles II dish in pewter, 16¾in. diam. circa 1674. $1,890 £1,050

One of a pair of broad rimmed dishes by James Taudin, 14½in. diam., circa 1690. $2,160 £1,200

(Sotheby's)

18th century flagon of baluster form with domed cover, 10½in. high.
$180 £90

(King & Chasemore)

Swiss pewter miniature wine flagon, circa 1800-1850, 5¾in. high. $200 £100

Late 18th century, German pewter flagon, 9in. high. $200 £100

French pewter miniature flagon, circa 1800-20, 3½in. high. $250 £125

Late 18th century, German bulbous shaped flagon, 11in. high. $270 £135

Late 18th century, Continental pewter flagon, 11in. high. $290 £145

Continental pewter wine flagon, circa 1760-70, 9in. high. $350 £175

35

FLAGONS

Scottish pewter flagon, 18th century, interior base marked with a Tudor rose with crown and Edinburgh, 8½in. $400 £200

One of a pair of 19th century pewter communion flagons, with embossed panel designs, and beaded borders, 12½in. high. $400 £200

Early 19th century Normandy flagon.
$450 £225

Flemish pear-shaped flagon by JVA, circa 1800, 25.5cm. high. $502 £260

Heavy lidded pewter flagon.
$504 £280

18th century flagon with attractive hinged lid, made by J. Weber of Zurich. $570 £285

36

18th century pewter Normandy flagon, 12in. high. $570 £285
(King & Chasemore)

FLAGONS

Early 18th century Scottish church
flagon. $620 £310

Pewter Guernsey pot flagon of typical
pear shape. $612 £340

Mid 17th century wine flagon by Jacob
Valin of Geneva, the collar surmounted
by a heart-shaped cover, with twin
acorn thumbpiece. $750 £375

Small George III flagon by I. & H., 10in
high, circa 1780. $772 £400

Fine cylindrical pewter flagon by Jonas
Durand, circa 1720, 16½in. high.
                           $720 £400

Dutch wine flagon of bulbous form,
18th century, 11in. high, inscribed
W.D.C. $756 £420

Early 18th century pewter flagon, 10¾in. high.   \$936 £520
(Christie's)

A rare Charles II flagon, 11.1/8in. tall, circa 1680. $936 £520
(Sotheby's)

18th century wine flagon with a cast medallion inside the base, 12¼in. tall. $1,100 £550

James I flagon with plain slightly tapering drum raised on an ovolo moulded foot, 34.5cm. high, circa 1610. $1,240 £620

Early 17th century cylindrical lidded flagon with scroll handle and open-shaped thumbpiece, bearing the rubbed touch mark on the handle of 'G.E.' $1,350 £675

A good flat lidded pewter flagon by 'W.W.', circa 1690. $1,400 £700

Large wine flagon by Andre Utin of Vevey, dated on the handle, 13½in. tall. $1,700 £850

A James I flagon of small size dated 1614, with erect notched thumbpiece. $1,700 £850

One of a pair of Queen Anne church flagons for Dumfries Kirk,
27in. high, circa 1705. $1,700 £850
(Sotheby's)

Pair of Queen Anne church flagons by Adam Banks of Milngate, 27cm. high, circa 1705. $1,900 £950

Fine and rare Charles I pewter flagon, circa 1640, 12in. high. $1,834 £950

Charles 11 Beefeater flagon by R.B., 10.5/8in. tall, circa 1675.
$2,300 £1,150

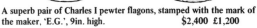

A superb pair of Charles I pewter flagons, stamped with the mark of the maker, 'E.G.', 9in. high. $2,400 £1,200

FLAGONS

James I flagon of plain drum and ovolo moulded foot and lip, 13½in. high, circa 1610. $2,400 £1,200

North German pewter flagon by H. Helmoke of Lubeck, circa 1656. $2,600 £1,300

A fine Stuart flagon by John Emes, 11¼in. high, circa 1680. $2,600 £1,300

Charles I bun shaped covered flagon. $2,800 £1,400

A fine Beefeater flagon by Francis Seagood, 9¾in. high, circa 1600. $2,900 £1,450

One of a pair of late Stuart flagons by W. W., 9½in. high, circa 1690. $3,000 £1,500

A rare Charles I flagon of slender tapering form by T.P., 11½in. tall, circa 1625. $3,600 £1,800

(Sotheby's)

Late 18th century German flask, 8¾in. high, in pewter. $756 £420
(Christie's)

Small Victorian pewter flask, 3½in.
diameter. $6 £3

Late 19th century pewter hip flask.
                              $8 £4

GLOCKENKANNE

A Swiss Glockenkanne, inscribed
1748, 25cm. high. $750 £375

18th century pewter Glockenkanne,
made in Zurich. $950 £475

GOBLETS

A small, early 19th century pewter
goblet. $30 £15

Late 18th century pewter chalice,
7in. high. $150 £75

47

Early 17th century German or Swiss pewter Guild Hanap, 25½in.
high. $1,500 £750
(Christie's, New York)

Late 19th century pewter capstan
inkwell. $30 £15

An unusual 19th century soft metal
inkwell. $60 £30

An early pewter banded stoneware
inkwell. $200 £100

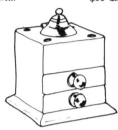

Pewter cube-form inkstand, the base
inscribed 'Coutts Banking House,
1790'. $400 £200

JARDINIERES

A small late 19th century Art Nouveau
style pewter jardiniere . $60 £30

An 18th century oval fluted pewter
jardiniere. $850 £425

49

JUGS

Late 19th century pewter jug, 6in. high. $16 £8

Victorian milk jug with a pewter lid. $20 £10

A Victorian Britannia metal vase shaped wine jug. $30 £15

Victorian soft metal hot water jug with embossed decoration. $40 £20

A small, squat, 18th century pewter jug. $50 £25

Liberty & Co. polished pewter water jug , circa 1910. $80 £40

An early 19th century embossed pewter jug. $130 £65

A pewter oviform four gallon jug, 16½in. high. $150 £75

A 19th century ale jug with domed cover, 9in. high. $150 £75

Lidless pewter jug with sieve, 8½in. high, inscribed 'Crown Broad Place in Holland Mill', half gallon capacity, circa 1780. $320 £160

An Oxford pewter ale or cider jug of quart capacity, circa 1800. $400 £200

Pewter pear-shaped wine pitcher, French, circa 1800, 25.5cm. high. $579 £300

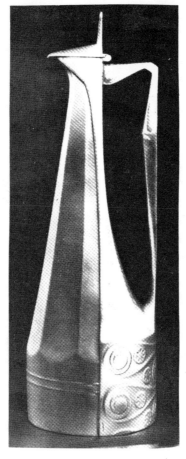

Edelzinn pewter jug, circa 1901, 33.5cm. high. $2,775   £1,500
(Sotheby's)

Victorian pewter, baluster pint measure. $36 £18

A 19th century baluster shaped pewter quart measure. $52 £26

19th century Scottish pewter lidded measure. $60 £30

19th century half pint measure.
$60 £30

19th century baluster pewter quart measure by James Yates, 6½in. high. $64 £32

A 19th century pewter quart measure with nicely shaped handle. $70 £35

MEASURES

Late 19th century thistle measure with Glasgow tree. $70 £35

Large 19th century lidded Scottish measure. $80 £40

A very fine pewter pint measure in the form of a spouted tankard, with fish tail handle, by Edwards, Clerkenwell Road, circa 1840, 5in. high.$100 £50

A French demi litre cylindrical measure, 7in. high. $110 £55

A graduated set of four 19th century pewter baluster shaped measures. $110 £55

19th century baluster shaped measure with scroll thumbpiece, 10in. high. $110 £55

(King & Chasemore)

MEASURES

French 19th century pewter, lidded litre measure, 8in. $110 £55

A Victorian baluster quart measure from the Lincoln Arms, Kings Cross. $120 £60

Late 18th century bulbous measure. $130 £65

19th century French litre measure, 9in. high stamped D.A. et Cie. $150 £75

18th century Continental measure of Normandy type, 8¼in. high. $150 £75

19th century French demi litre measure, by Oudard Rudot, 6¾in. high. $160 £80

19th century French litre measure, by Humbert Leclerc a Lisle, 8½in. high.
$190 £95

18th century pewter measure, handle engraved, by N. Jodard, 10¾in. high.
$230 £115

Set of Irish haystack measures in pewter. $230 £115

French 19th century pewter, lidded, double litre measure, 10in. $240 £120

18th century Continental measure, 10½in. high. $240 £120

Early 19th century one gallon harvest measure with scroll handle, 11½in.
high. $280 £140

(King & Chasemore)

One of a collection of seven graduated pewter spirit measures. $280 £140

English pewter pint measure by John Warne, circa 1850, 5in. high. $280 £140

Late 19th century German measure inscribed 'M' and dated 1891, by Joseph Schiller, 12¼in. high.
$280 £140

Domed lidded measure of quart capacity in pewter, 7½in. high, circa 1800.
$350 £175

French lidded cylindrical measure, 19th century, 11in. high. $360 £200

Jersey pewter wine measure of typical form, about 5½in. high. $420 £210

MEASURES

Lidless pewter half gallon measure, 7½in. high, circa 1820. $420 £210

19th century French double litre measure by Bunel a Villedieu-le-Poeles, 10¾in. high. $450 £225

Rare Channel Islands lidded pot measure, 10¾in. high. $432 £240

Early 18th century bulbous shaped pewter measure, probably German, circa 1719. $560 £280

Guernsey lidded quart measure, 9in. high, by A. Carter, mid 18th century. $540 £300

A bulbous 18th century pewter measure. $650 £325

Late 18th century baluster measure of pint capacity, by Randall Moring,
6¼in. high. $579 £300

(Sotheby's)

Bud baluster measure of half pint capacity, by John Carr, touch dated
1697, 5¼in. tall. $680 £340

(Sotheby's)

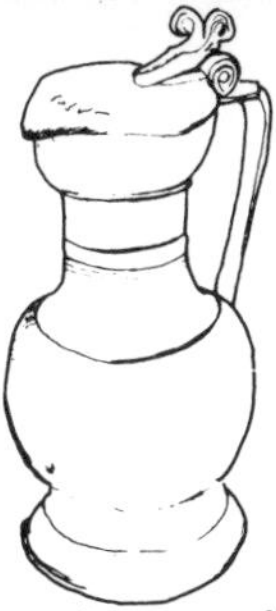

18th century wine measure by Andre Utin of Vevey. $680 £340

Guernsey lidded pot measure in pewter, mid 18th century, by A. Carter, 11¼in. high. $684 £380

A Scots baluster measure of quart capacity by William Scott of Edinburgh, 20cm. high, circa 1800. $800 £400

An Irish pewter gallon measure by J. Austen. $900 £450

A rare Irish gallon haystack measure by William Seymour, 29.5cm. high, circa 1825. $1,000 £500

A rare Scottish, pear-shaped half gallon measure, 10¼in. high. $1,000 £500

One of a set of three French 18th century pewter measures.

$1,000 £500

(King & Chasemore)

A fine set of three, mid 18th century, pewter baluster shaped measures, quart, pint and half pint. $1,080 £540

Set of seven pewter haystack measures, 3in. to 11½in. high. $1,500 £750

Baluster shaped wine measure of gallon capacity by Thomas Stevens of London, 33.2cm. high, circa 1735. $1,800 £900

65

A gallon size bud measure with maker's mark E.S., 12¾in. high, circa
1680. $2,000 £1,000

(Sotheby's)

An Oriental pewter circular spice jar
and cover, 7½in. high. $36 £18

Pewter pint mug with reeded band
and base stamped WR, 15½cm. high.
$90 £45

Early 20th century pewter letter rack
decorated with coloured stones, 14in.
wide. $70 £35

Pewter Art Nouveau lady leaning over
lily pond, 7in. high. $70 £35

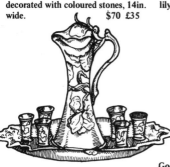

WMF silvered metal liqueur set and tray,
circa 1900. $463 £240

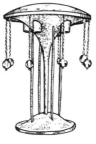

Good, Wiener werkstatte electroplated
metal and glass table lamp, circa 1905,
43.5cm. high. $7,334 £3,800

67

MISCELLANEOUS

Early 20th century pewter napkin ring. $4 £2

Gallia cruet set, 8cm. high, in silvered metal, 1920's. $157 £85

Unusual enamelled pendant on silver coloured metal, 5cm. long, circa 1905. $222 £120

20th century pewter sugar caster, 7in. high. $16 £8

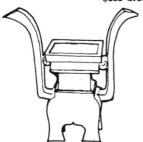

19th century Japanese pewter Ting, 28½cm. $80 £40

Rare Queen Anne period pewter mace. $550 £275

A miniature polished pewter firegrate with Royal coat-of-arms, circa 1820, 11in. wide, 15in. high. $100 £50

Attractive Art Nouveau walking stick with silvered metal top, German, circa 1900. $106 £55

An oval Britannia metal meat cover, stamped James Dixon and Sons, Sheffield, 10in. wide. $30 £15

A pewter spoon rack by A. Heiddan, Lubeck, circa 1820. $320 £160

18th century pewter 'Welsh Hat' liner. $160 £80

Art Nouveau pewter sugar basin with floral decoration. $30 £15

One of a pair of 20th century Chinese pewter horse-heads, 16in. high.
$130 £65

(King and Chasemore)

A small , 20th century, hammered
pewter mirror, 10in. high. $20 £10

Early 20th century, pewter framed
mirror decorated with coloured
stones, 15in. high. $100 £50

Hammered pewter mirror with blue
enamel decoration. $240 £120

Art Deco mirror glass clock, 1930's,
33.75cm. long. $370 £200

Guernardeau patinated metal Art
Nouveau mirror frame, circa 1900,
41.5cm. high. $463 £250

WMF Art Nouveau silvered metal frame,
36cm. high, circa 1900. $965 £500

PICHET

French pewter pichet or wine measure, circa 1735-50. $624 £330
(Sotheby's)

Mid 18th century pewter pitcher.
$200 £100

Dome topped pewter pitcher.
$324 £180

An English pewter cider pitcher, of
rare pint size, with domed cover,
scroll handle and open thumbpiece.
$360 £180

18th century Continental pewter
baluster pitcher. $700 £350

18th century Swiss pewter wine
pitcher, 11in. high. $800 £400

18th century Bar-Sur-Aube pewter
wine pitcher, 30cm. high.
$1,250 £625

PLATES

18th century pewter plate by Bush and Perkins, 9¾in. diameter. $40 £20

A pewter plate with scroll border, the centre with embossed crest and motto, 9in. diameter. $60 £30

A 19th century pewter circular plate, engraved with monogram, 9¾in. $80 £40

Deep, German pewter plate with single touch mark of angel holding scales and crown above, 9in. diameter. $90 £45

A French pewter circular plate with reeded and wave border, the centre with a crown and fleur de lys, 10½in. diameter. $90 £45

19th century plate with waved border, 9¼in. diameter. $100 £50

18th century Continental plate, with moulded rim, 11¼in. diameter.
$100 £50

An early pewter plate with touch mark, crowned rose, 11¾in. diameter.
$100 £50

One of a pair of 19th century deep circular pewter plates with moulded rims, 14in. diameter. $150 £75

A French pewter plate, ownership marks I.D.B., 13in. diameter.
$170 £85

Wavy edged oval pewter meat platter, 14½in. long. $180 £95

18th century pewter plate, 16in. diameter. $260 £130

A Stuart plate with narrow triple reeded rim by Thomas Templeman,
8½in. diameter, 17th century. $260 £130
(Sotheby's)

A pewter plate, circa 1730, 15in.
diameter. $260 £130

Queen Anne plate with gadrooned
border by John Shorey, 9in. diam.,
circa 1710. $234 £130

A pair of late 18th century embossed pewter plates. $260 £130

A Stuart plate, maker's mark R.B.,
8.7/8in. diameter, late 17th century.
            $260 £130

A plain rimmed Stuart plate by Richard
Fletcher, 9¼in. diameter, circa 1690.
            $320 £160

PLATES

A wriggled work plate with single reeded rim by Chapman, 7.7/8in. diameter, circa 1720. $360 £180

A fine wavy-edged plate by Thomas Chamberlain, 9½in. diameter, circa 1760. $420 £210

One of a set of three pewter soup plates, 9¾in. diam. $454 £240

One of a pair of English pewter flat rim plates, circa 1709, 10in. diam. $500 £2

One of a pair of Stuart plates by Edward Kent, 9½in. diameter, circa 1690. $500 £250

One of a pair of octagonal pewter plates by George Bacon, circa 1750-60. $540 £280

A Charles II wriggled work plate with narrow rim, maker F.B., 8½in.
diameter, circa 1665.   **$600 £300**

(Sotheby's)

One of a set of four George II pewter soup plates by Robert Massam,
London 1736, 9¾in. diameter. $600 £300
(Christie's, New York)

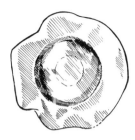

16th century pewter plate or saucer, 7½in. diam. (damaged) $695 £360

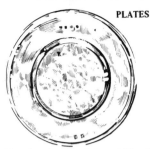

One of a pair of broad rimmed 'Mount Edgecumbe' plates by W.H., 9¾in. diameter, circa 1670. $880 £440

A wriggled work marriage plate by James Hitchman, engraved with a peacock, 8¼in. diameter, circa 1718. $900 £450

A large broad rimmed plate made by Edward Everett, 11¾in. diameter, circa 1660. $1,160 £580

A fine broad rimmed paten by T.B., 9in. diameter, circa 1670. $1,200 £600

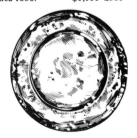

Charles II broad rimmed paten by the maker I.I., 9¼in. diameter, circa 1670. $1,360 £680

PLATES

One of a set of ten pewter dinner plates, 9¾in. diam. $1,399 £740

Rare wriggled work plate, circa 1695, 8½in. diam. $1,544 £800

Pair of wriggled work marriage plates by Thomas Widmore, 8½in. diameter, circa 1715. $1,600 £800

One of a set of twelve early 18th century octagonal pewter plates with moulded rims by Thomas Chamberlain. $3,000 £1,500

18th century pewter plate from a set of twenty-two. $3,200 £1,600

One of a pair of wriggled work plates by James Hitchman, 9in. diam.
$3,200 £1,600

(Sotheby's)

PLAQUES

A cast pewter plaque of a trotting horse, circa 1830, 11¼in. long, 8in. high.   **$70 £35**

One of a pair of cast soft metal swans, which when placed together make a complete swan pub sign, 13in. high.   **$150 £75**

Pewter relief of 'The Battle of Rocroi', signed Reuerand, 1859, 12.5cm. x 7.5cm.   **$150 £75**

Silvered metal plaque 'The Spirit of Christmas', by John G. Hardy, circa 1895, 41cm. long.   **$241 £130**

PRISMEN KANN

Octagonal pewter Swiss wine can, early 19th century, 26.5cm. high.   **$643 £340**

Pewter Prismen Kann or lidded flask, by F. Cane, Appenzell, Swiss, early 19th century, 36cm. high. **$750 £375**

Fine late William and Mary posset pot in pewter, 9½in. wide, circa 1695.
$4,320 £2,400

(Sotheby's)

Very rare pair of Queen Anne relief cast pewter porringers by John
Quick, London, 18.4cm. across, circa 1710. $5,400 £3,000
(Sotheby's)

A porringer with booged sides and gutter and boss in the base by John Langford, 7¼in. diam., circa 1725.
$440 £220

Charles II porringer of booged type, 7.1/8in. diameter, circa 1680.
$560 £280

Porringer with finely pierced and shaped ear by Adam Banks of Chester, 7½in. diam., circa 1700.
$560 £280

A good Stuart porringer of booged type, 7.7/8in. diam., circa 1690.
$600 £300

A Charles II porringer, with single fretted ear, 7¼in. diam., circa 1675.
$1,040 £520

Charles II porringer with flat bottom by W.I., 7.7/8in. diam., circa 1670.
$1,200 £600

SALTS

Small Victorian pewter salt on shaped legs. $8 £4

An octagonal salt with concave sides and oval salt depression, 3in. long, circa 1720. $240 £120

Trencher salt of squat form, 1½in. high, circa 1700. $260 £130

A rare trencher salt of bulbous type with incised reeding around waist, 1¾in. high, circa 1700. $320 £160

Trencher salt with cylindrical sides maker's mark I.H., 1½in. high, circa 1700. $360 £180

One of a pair of William and Mary capstan salts, 2¼in. high, circa 1690. $1,080 £600

Small late Victorian spelter figure of a cricketer. $40 £20

A pair of French bronze spelter female figures of 'Gaiete and Modeste', on ebonised plinths, 12in. high. $70 £35

Whitbread counter model of a spelter figure, 1ft.4in. high, circa 1930. $80 £40

Art Nouveau gilt metal figure of a girl dancer, 11in. $100 £50

An Art Nouveau coloured metal figure of a girl and a pillar, on onyx base, 11in. high. $100 £50

A small late 19th century bust of Judith, 7in. high. $120 £60

SPELTER FIGURES

Art Nouveau spelter bust, signed, circa 1900. $200 £100

Pair of Art Deco gilded metal figures of dancers, 14½in. $230 £115

Spelter figure of a girl on an onyx and marble base, circa 1920, 1ft.6in. long. $260 £130

Silvered metal female figure, signed Fayral. $540 £270

Late 19th century French bronzed spelter figure of a Harlequin, 38in. tall. $700 £350

Painted white metal Chiparus group of woman and goats. $1,100 £550

A rare medieval spoon with lion statant gardant top, 12.1cm. long, 15th century. $440 £220

(Sotheby's)

SPOONS

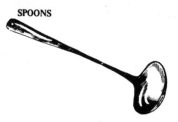

Large Victorian pewter ladle. $30 £15

Continental pewter spoon with rat tail on back, 6in. long, early 17th century. $140 £70

A slit top spoon with maker's mark ?L. stamped in bowl, 6in. long, 16th century. $140 £70

16th century Latten spoon of St. Andrew with cross sattire, 12.6cm. long.
$145 £75

16th century Latten spoon of the Virgin and Child, 13.5cm. long. $145 £75

17th century Latten spoon of St. Peter with key, 14.1cm. long. $212 £110

16th century baluster knopped spoon, 6¼in. long. $240 £120

Hexagonal knopped spoon struck in bowl with R.B., 6½in. long, 16th century. $290 £145

A slit top spoon with hexagonal stem, touch mark E.H., 6½in. long, circa 1600. $300 £150

16th century acorn knopped spoon with round stem, touch mark R.N., 6½in. long. $340 £170

A hexagon knopped spoon with hexagonal stem, touch mark R.G., dated 1632, 6½in. long. $420 £210

A relief cast Queen Anne portrait spoon, with initials S.S., 7¼in. long, circa 1702. $520 £260

STEGKANNE

A good Swiss stegkanne, the cover with winged thumbpiece, 32cm. high, 18th century. $3,100 £1,550

A Bernese stegkanne by Daniel Hemman from the first half of the 18th century, 31.5cm. high.
$3,100 £1,550

A William IV pint tankard with
double scroll handle. $40 £20

A George IV quart tankard with
horizontal reeded bands. $48 £24

Cylindrical pewter tankard stamped
on rim 'T.J. Birch, Pint'. $50 £25

A 19th century engraved pewter
pint tankard, with glass base.
$50 £25

19th century pewter tankard.
$50 £25

19th century pewter half pint tankard.
$56 £28

19th century quart tankard of baluster form with scroll handle and
spout, 6½in. high.   **$60 £30**
                        (King & Chasemore)

Victorian pint tankard of tapering cylindrical form, with scroll handle
and spout, 4½in. high. $70 £35
(King & Chasemore)

A half pint, glass bottomed pewter tankard, with the touch mark of Townsend and Compton, circa 1810. $70 £35

19th century pewter quart tankard. $80 £40

Late 18th century pewter quart tankard with mock silver hall marks. $80 £40

19th century tulip shaped pewter tankard. $80 £40

One of a pair of half pint tulip shaped pewter tankard, by Joseph Morgan of Bristol, and with Customs and Excise mark for Carlisle, 3½in. high. $80 £40

A heavy pint pewter ale tankard, with the touch mark of C. Bentley, circa 1840, 5in. high. $80 £40

Victorian half pint tankard of baluster form, the domed cover with
shell thumbpiece, 4¾in. high. $90 £45
(King & Chasemore)

Early 19th century Scottish quart tankard, by J. McGlashan & Co., Glasgow. $100 £50

Small pewter Continental lidded tankard. $99 £55

18th century pewter lipped tankard. $120 £60

A fine late 18th century pewter tankard. $120 £60

19th century lidded pewter tankard with glass bottom and open arched thumbpiece to double domed lid, 7½in. high. $120 £60

A late Georgian pewter pint tankard with nicely shaped handle. $120 £60

TANKARDS

Early 19th century quart tankard by Joseph Morgan, Bristol, 6½in. high. $150 £75

18th century German pewter lidded tankard. $200 £100

19th century Swedish tapering lidded pewter tankard with ball thumbpiece. $260 £130

19th century pewter straight sided tankard, with lid and curled decorated thumbpiece. $280 £140

18th century pewter mounted pottery tankard. $300 £150

German pewter tankard with broad foot. $400 £200

German pewter tankard, 10in. tall with engraved body. $500 £250

Dome topped pewter stein.
$468 £260

Swedish or Baltic pewter tankard with flat top and ball thumbpiece, 18th century, 8in. high. $520 £260

Late 17th century pewter tankard.
$550 £275

Early 19th century German tankard inscribed M. Heydanin, 1808, the body engraved with three oval panels, 9½in. high, by Friedrich Ferdinand Braune, Kamenz. $550 £275

Pewter lidded tankard with scroll thumbpiece , circa 1730. $540 £300

TANKARDS

18th century pewter flat topped
tankard with ball thumbpiece.
$600 £300

Scandinavian lidded pewter peg
tankard, 7in. high, circa 1760.
$600 £300

Scandinavian pewter peg tankard.
$600 £300

A William and Mary pewter tankard,
with the maker's mark 'I.B.', circa
1690. $700 £350

A Queen Anne tankard by Adam Banks
of Milngate, the drum encircled by a
single fillet at waist, 17.5cm high, circa
1710. $780 £390.

Mid 18th century Swiss pewter tankard.
$794 £420

Early Georgian pewter tankard by Richard Going, 6½in. high, circa 1725. $720 £400
(Sotheby's)

TANKARDS

Austrian spouted pewter tankard, circa 1702, 18cm. high. $794 £420

18th century lidded pewter tankard, 9in. high. $840 £420

Early Georgian pewter tankard by Richard Going, Bristol, circa 1725, 6½in. high. $864 £480

Stuart period lidded tankard, circa 1685, 8in. tall. $1,000 £500

Rare Saxon pewter tankard, probably by Hans Wildt the younger, 6¼in. high, circa 1590-1600. $936 £520

Good, George II domed pewter lidded tankard by William Eddon, circa 1725-40, 7in. high. $1,077 £570

Plain Stuart flat-lidded pewter tankard by LS, circa 1680, 7½in. high.
$1,044 £580

(Sotheby's)

William and Mary pewter tankard with high domed cover, 7in. high, circa 1695. $1,116 £620

(Sotheby's)

A cylindrical pewter tankard from
the first half of the 17th century.
$1,300 £650

Fine George I pewter tankard by John
Spicer, circa 1720, 7in. high.
$1,350 £750

Charles II wriggled work tankard by
I. I. 6¾in. high, circa 1680.
$2,250 £1,250

Rare Cromwellian pewter tankard with
a wide flared foot, 9¾in. tall.
$3,200 £1,600

Fine small Charles II wriggled work
tankard by LA, 6in. high, circa 1680.
$3,600 £2,000

Important William and Mary wriggled
work pewter tankard, maker's mark RS,
6½in. high overall, circa 1690.
$4,320 £2,400

Pewter quart tappit hen measure.
(Locke & England)

£684 £380

Small, Victorian pewter tappit hen.
$60 £30

19th century pewter tappit hen with London touch mark, 10in. high.
$80 £40

A large 19th century pewter tappit hen. $150 £75

Mid 18th century George III pewter tappit hen, Guernsey, 9in. high.
$250 £125

Late 18th century Scottish pewter tappit hen, 10¼in. high. $250 £125

One of a set of five 19th century pewter measures of tappit hen type, 8½in. high. $320 £160

109

TAPPIT HENS

Pewter mutchkin tappit hen.
$441 £245

Large 18th century Scottish pewter tappit hen measure. $520 £260

Late 18th century tappit hen of unusual waisted form with domed cover. $560 £280

Late 18th century Scottish pewter uncrested tappit hen measure, 10¼in. high. $540 £300

A pewter tappit hen with domed cover and thumbpiece, 12in. high.
$800 £400

A pewter tappit hen, with threaded bands and engraved I.W.M.H., 12in. high. $800 £400

Scots crested tappit hen shaped measure, 18th century, 9¾in. high.
$772 £400

(Sothcby's)

TAVERN POTS

Large pewter lidless tavern pot, 6¾in. high, circa 1710-15. $504 £280

Rare lidless pewter tavern pot by IG, 5in. high, circa 1720-30. $684 £380

TAZZA

Victorian, Britannia metal tazza, 8in. high. $70 £35

Pewter fruit tazza, about 1905, 10½in. high. $72 £40

Large metal tazza, 44cm. high, WMF marks, 1900-1910. $333 £180

WMF silvered metal and glass tazza, circa 1900, 36.25cm. high. $481 £260

A small late 19th century soft metal three-piece teaset. $40 £20

Late 19th century Art Nouveau style three piece pewter
teaset. $100 £50

Liberty & Co. 'Tudric' pewter tea service, after 1903, designed by
Archibald Knox. $407 £220

TEAPOTS

Late 19th century Britannia metal
teapot. $24 £12

Late Victorian engraved soft metal
teapot. $30 £15

Late 19th century pewter teapot of
square form. $36 £18

A large Victorian pear shaped fluted
pewter teapot. $40 £20

A nicely shaped Victorian pewter
teapot with an ebony handle.
                           $70 £35

Stylish Art Deco teapot in silver-coloured
metal, 1930's, 11.5cm. high. $251 £130

English pewter tobacco jar, stamped
Alderson, circa 1850, 4½in. high.
$160 £80

Oval, 19th century, pewter tobacco
jar. $180 £90

TUREENS

18th century pewter tureen on claw
and ball feet. $320 £160

Pewter oval tureen by John Jones,
late 19th century. $900 £450

One of a pair of circular pewter
tureens and covers, 18th century.
$900 £450

Oval pewter soup tureen and cover,
18¾in. long. $1,021 £540

TRAYS

Late 19th century soft metal card tray. $40 £20

Late 19th century Art Nouveau style pewter tray. $150 £75

URNS

An unusual Toleware tea urn with pewter scroll double handles and finial knob to lid, circa 1830, 17in. overall height. $180 £90

Late 18th century pewter water cistern with tap, 9in. high. $300 £150

WINE FUNNELS

George III pewter wine funnel, circa 1820, 5in. high, 3¾in. diam. $50 £25

Pewter wine funnel with goblet-shaped body and copper hanging ring to rim, 6½in. high. $70 £35

English pewter quart cann, circa 1840, 6¼in. high. $200 £100

18th century Normandy pitchet of shouldered form 11¾in. high. $252 £140

English pewter footed cann stamped 1795, 6¼in. high. $300 £150

18th/19th century pewter Swiss Kelchkanne, 21.5cm. high. $540 £280

A good, Swiss wine can by Jakob Ganting, the bulbous body with floral decoration, 33.2cm. high, 18th century. $1,600 £800

Swiss pewter Bauchkanne by Antoni Storno of Brig. $1,800 £1,000

WINE VESSELS

An early Georgian pewter wine vessel. $48 £24

VASES

Late 19th century soft metal epergne. $30 £15

An unusual pewter wine vessel, 27in. high. $360 £200

Late 19th century German pewter vase. $30 £15

German clear glass vase in a silver plated pewter case by Crivit. $40 £20

Early 20th century Art Nouveau pewter vase, 5in. high. $44 £22

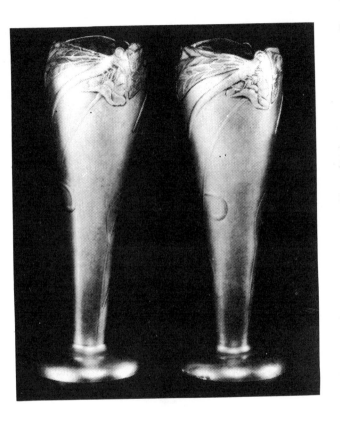

One of a pair of Liberty & Co pewter vases, after 1903, 19cm
high. $68   £35
(Sotheby Belgravia)

Liberty & Co. pewter vase, 35cm. high, after 1903. $77 £40
(Sotheby Belgravia)

Desny silvered metal vase, 22cm. high, 1930's, with ebonised wood handles.
$315 £170

Attractive Puiforcat vase, 1930's, 10.75cm. high, in silver coloured metal.
$333 £180

Stylish Puiforcat vase and cover, 20cm. high, 1930's.
$352 £190

Puiforcat vase, 1930's, in silver coloured metal, 14.25cm. high.
$407 £220

A pair of Jean Dunand patinated metal vases on tripod bases, circa 1920-25 , 25.5cm. high.
$1,073 £580

121

INDEX